The Whitley _____

The Whitley Lectureship was first established in 1949. It was begun in honour of W.T. Whitley (1861-1947), arguably the first systematic modern Baptist historian. Whitley was a notable scholar and a servant of the Church of Christ. He had pastorates in England and Australia. He served the denomination in both countries in many ways, including pursuing historical studies.

Whitley was a key figure in the formation of the Baptist Historical Society (1908). He edited its journal which soon gained an international reputation for the quality of its contents. Altogether he made a particularly remarkable contribution to Baptist life and self-understanding, providing an inspiring model of how a pastor scholar might enrich the life and faith of others.

The establishment of the Lectureship in his name was intended to be an encouragement to research by Baptist scholars into aspects of Christian life and thought and to enable the results of such research to be published and available to the denomination and beyond.

The Whitley Lectureship's Management Committee is composed of representatives of the Baptist Colleges, the Baptist Union of Great Britain, the Baptist Missionary Society, the Baptist Ministers Fellowship and the Baptist Historical Society.

Through the years the encouragement towards scholarship has taken different forms, from the full support of the writing of lectures for publication by a designated Whitley Lecturer to the making available of smaller grants to those working at particular research interests.

In 1996 the Management Committee of the Whitley Lectureship began a new initiative in keeping with the original purpose. It was agreed to appoint each year a Lecturer to write and deliver a lecture as a contribution to scholarly Baptist thought. Each lecture will be published.

We are delighted that the second lecture in this new series is given by the Revd Ruth Gouldbourne. She was a local minister in Bedford before becoming a tutor at the Bristol Baptist College. She has taken up a theme which remains challenging for Baptists and is important for all Christians.

Brian Haymes
on behalf of the Management Committee

THE WHITLEY LECTURE
1997-1998

REINVENTING THE WHEEL
Women and Ministry
in English Baptist Life

Ruth M.B. Gouldbourne

Whitley Publications

The Author and Whitley Publications 1997

ISBN 0-9528150-3-6

Whitley Publications
c/o Regent's Park College
Pusey Street
Oxford
OX1 2LB
England

THE WHITLEY LECTURE
1997-1998

REINVENTING THE WHEEL
Women and Ministry in English Baptist Life

Ruth M.B. Gouldbourne

There are two reasons why I am particularly glad to be invited to offer this year's Whitley Lecture. The first is, in view of the topic I have been invited to consider, that this year marks the end of the Churches Decade of Solidarity with Women - not an event that has set our Baptist churches alight with enthusiasm or renewal, but something which has been, for some of us at least, of great importance. Secondly, and this is why I in particular am glad to be doing this, rather than simply glad the lecture is being done, I spent a couple of years as the patrol leader in a Baptist Guide Company in Edinburgh where one of my patrol was the great-granddaughter of Dr W.T. Whitley. It seems appropriate that the connection should be through the female side, and that it should have been in Guides, an organization which allowed me scope as a girl to explore activities often associated with boys - camping, exploring, leadership - while still insisting that female leadership, organization and togetherness was important.

The subject I have been invited to consider is women and ministry in Baptist life, and again I count myself lucky in being peculiarly qualified for this - I am a woman who has experienced ministry within the Baptist movement in Britain, I am a woman who exercises recognized ministry within the Baptist movement in England, and I am a woman who has the privilege of reflecting on recognized ministry within the Baptist movement in England, as I teach in one of our Colleges. In the light of all this, it is both with excitement and with trepidation that I approach the topic - excitement, because this is the exploration in some way of my own story; trepidation, because in places this is a painful story.

I want to start with some reflections on the topic itself. Firstly, what do we mean when as Baptists, we speak of ministry. I am fairly sure we do not mean - at least, I know I do not mean, only those who have been ordained, or who are on the accredited list. We are committed to a theology of the priesthood of all believers, which must say something about the role in ministry of each believer. So, although at times in this lecture I will speak directly about the ordained ministry, I hope as well to look at this wider understanding, in which ministry is something Christ does in and through the church - that is, the gathered community of believers.

Secondly, I want to point out an oddity in the statement of the topic itself - women and ministry in Baptist life. Since I have become involved in gender studies, it has become borne in upon me that when we have a question of gender, what we have is a 'women's' problem - the debate for example is 'should mothers go out to work?' - not, 'should fathers stay at home?', or 'how can a political party, whichever one it is, attract the female vote' - often linked, incidentally to the good looks or otherwise of the candidates, rather than what are the patterns that determine male voting? The assumption which creates this pattern is that men are normal, and women are somehow a slightly off-centre part of the species for whom certain concessions must be made, since they cannot fit the normality. So, I am afraid to say, is it the case with the topic - women and ministry, set as different categories; this puts women alongside a context which doesn't include them. What I hope to show here is that ministry has always included women, but that the form of inclusion might be well worth reflecting on, as much for what it says about ministry as about women.

These are the reflections on the topic I was given - the title I have chosen for myself, and this is why. I believe passionately in history, not simply because it is a fascinating subject, but because it is a source of power. One of the issues I have faced in all my experiences of ministry - receiving, doing and thinking - has been the overwhelming sense that, as a woman, I was doing something new and unusual. That is at once an exciting and a disempowering experience. It is exciting because it means there is the chance to do something new - but it is disempowering because there is no story, no ground on which to stand, nobody to look to for identity - no history. One of the things which feminists have taught us is that there is a history of women, that women have been around, active and thinking for as long as men, and that we need to hear this story. Adrienne Rich has written this:

> The entire history of women's struggle for self determination has been muffled in silence over and over ... each feminist work has tended to be received as if it emerged from nowhere; as if each of us lived and thought and worked without any historical past or contextual present. This is one of the ways in which women's work and thinking has been made to seem sporadic, errant, orphaned of any tradition of its own. In fact we do have a long feminist tradition both oral and written, which has built on itself over and over, recovering essential elements even when these have been strangled or wiped out ... Each contemporary feminist [is] attacked or dismissed *ad*

feminam, as if her politics were just an outburst of personal bitterness or rage.[1]

In our history, there have been women involved in all sorts of ministry, giving and receiving and thinking, but we have often lost the story or have not known what sort of questions we should ask. And so we have stood alone instead of together, reinventing the wheel, instead of allowing it to take us somewhere new.

There will be three areas covered in this lecture - a retelling of the story of women, and particularly women in ministry of various sorts in our Baptist life; the ministry that has been offered to women; and reflections on what it means to talk about women in ministry, however we define ministry. These will not be three discrete sections, but will be the questions I am hoping to address.

Two strands of early Baptists emerged out of the religious ferment of the late sixteenth and early seventeenth century - the General Baptists who came out of a group of Separatists who had emigrated to Holland in search of freedom, and the Particular Baptists whose origins were in Congregational churches which had remained in England. Although holding notions of church government and membership in common, the two groups were separated by a different understanding of the extent of salvation - Particular Baptists were Calvinists, whose theology was that Christ died only for the elect, while the Generals, influenced by the Dutchman Arminius held to a theology of general salvation - salvation for all who freely put their faith in Christ.

Thomas Helwys and some of the members of the Dutch contingent returned to England in 1612, and the first

General Baptist church on English soil was formed; in the 1630s, the first Particular Baptist congregation became separate from its parent Independent congregation. However, just because there were separate 'Baptist' congregations did not mean that all was cut and dried and clear. For a considerable time following this, there was significant coming and going and overlap between Baptist, Congregational and Quaker fellowships, so, in looking at what was going on in terms of ministry at this time, we are looking at a slightly broader canvas than simply 'Baptists' - we are looking at a ferment where new things were being thought, new shapes were being tried and new patterns were being developed.

In many of these Separatist churches - Congregational or Baptist - the first members were more women than men. In Bunyan Meeting in Bedford, for example, founded in 1650, before the arrival of John Bunyan into the fellowship, there were twelve original members, eight of them women. In the group which went to Holland, there seem to have been more women than men, and in the congregation from which the first General Baptist church emerged, there were also a majority of women. So what was going on?

The opponents of the Separatists were quite clear about what was happening - these heretical sects, as was always the case with heretical sects, were allowing women too much freedom and even power. Indeed, such movements could be seen to be heretical precisely because they allowed women to do what normal, orthodox believers would never dream of allowing. In this case, it appears that the opponents at least had the facts on their side - there were more women than men, and this had its effect on the way these new churches organized themselves. Keith Thomas presents it like this:

the upshot was that the separatist churches made considerable concessions to women in the sphere of church government.[2]

(This comment in itself, by the way, illustrates my point about women as this odd group to whom concessions must be made!). Those who were writing at the time also dealt with the issue, and so John Robinson, one of the leading early Separatists (who coined the words 'The Lord has yet more light and truth to break forth from his word') wrote:

It followeth necessarily that one faithful man, yea, or woman either, may as truly and effectually loose and bind, both in heaven and earth, as all the ministers in the world.[3]

John Smyth, who led that first congregation in Holland through its move from Separatism to full Baptist life, wrote:

women, servants and children admitted to full communion, yet under age [might] give voice in elections, excommunications and other public affairs of the church.

Such records as we have suggest that this was what happened. But why? Why were women being given, and not only being given but taking such a place? Part of the answer lies in the notion of the church with which these people were working. The whole impetus away from the old order and into separatism and then, for some, into Baptist life was that the church was not a machine through which grace flowed, controlled by the keepers of grace, the priests and bishops, but that the church was the gathered people of God - gathered by God, and each with a place and a responsibility before God for the whole. To be a member of such a church was dependent on the experience of the saving power of Christ, and admittance into membership required the expression of that experience. And this experience was not different for women and men. This is the necessity on which Robinson based his assertion about those who could effectually loose and bind - by being a part of the Church of God, one was a minister of God. This was the position of all believers, women and men.

Thus, those who criticised them were quite right - women did join the radical sects for the power and position which they attained, and so did the men. But this was not about seeking power for themselves, nor even about finding a place where power could be exercised in a society which denied it to all women and most men. Rather, it was the assertion of the belief that before God, there was only the status of baptized believer, there was no hierarchy of grace, and that within a church following such a pattern each person did have rights, a role and responsibilities: this is part of what it means to be a congregationally organized fellowship.

This is not to say, of course, that women were leaders in the churches. The names which have come down to us of recognized leaders - John Smyth, Thomas Helwys, Henry Jessey, William Kiffin - are all men. They were the recognized and approved leaders; there was no incipient feminist movement among our early Baptist ancestors. There was, however, a recognition that women had consciences which were also free. Once that is recognized, then certain things flow from it in terms of the being of the church and the right, or rather, necessity to speak.

In about 1639, Mrs Kelly, a widow, married Mr Hazzard, a clergyman who was lecturer at St Mary Redcliffe in Bristol, and was to be vicar at St Ewins in the same city. She would not conform and had openly in the presence of the congregation gone forth from his sermon when he began to assert that pictures and images might be used. In time Goodman Atkins, Goodman Cole Richard Moone and Mr Baconb, together with Mrs Hazzard became distressed at listening to Common Prayer. But before Mrs Hazzard could get out from that hearing of Common Prayer, she had a very sore conflict of her spirit, because her Husband did read that ... for it would go of ill report if she should forbear. Her conflict was resolved one morning, when, on being unable to decide whether to go to the service or not, she read Rev 14:9-11 which speaks of the punishment of those who bear the mark of the beast.

So in that year of our Lord - 1640 - those five persons ... at Mrs's Hazzard's house, at the upper end of Broad St in Bristol, they met together, and came to a holy Resolution to separate from the worship of the world and times they lived in, and that they would goe noe more to it, and with godly purpose of heart joyned themselves together in the Lord; and only this covenanting, That they would, in the strength and assistance of the Lord, come forth of the world and worship the Lord more purely, persevering therein to the end.[4]

It became part of the scandal thrown at the separatists that women took part, women even preached. There was Mrs Attaway, at the General Baptist Church in Bell Alley in Coleman Street in London. She started preaching to a group of women, but men soon joined - young men, apprentices and unrespectable people. The meetings were marked by much laughter and hilarity - and that was not the least of the scandal.

Thomas Edwards in *Gangraena* and *Six Women Preachers Discover'd*, speaks with the horror of all right-thinking men, who disapproved of such goings-on and saw them as marks of heresy, when he expresses his disgust at this laxity and unnatural behaviour. In these early years of Separatist and the Baptist life, women were taking part in ministry - preaching, speaking, voting, being converted, struggling alongside their men for the opportunity to follow the truth they had seen.

The responsibilities of belonging to this kind of church were taken seriously too, and the ministry which women received from the churches helps us to see how they were viewed - as individual responsible adults, who had their duties and privileges. The Fenstanton Records, one of those treasure houses of early Baptist history, give us some fascinating examples of the way in which women received ministry. For example, there was the widow Binns, from Over in Cambridgeshire, who found herself questioned by the Messenger about why she was attending the parish church. Her answer was that she was a friend of Mr Pope and it pleased him that she was there. The churches came to the conclusion that this was 'heinous sin' and admonished her. The Record goes on

> Then she alleged that she was forced to do so for the maintenance of herself and her children. We replied that was not the way to be maintained, but if it were, she ought not to have used it; for shall we do evil that good may come of it? God forbid. Then after many other words she confessed that she had done evil, and said that she was very sorry for it. Whereupon the congregation did willingly accept thereof and did receive her; and to manifest their love gave unto her seven shillings to satisfy her necessities.[5]

Then there was Jane Adams, who was questioned about why she did not attend the meetings, and answered that her husband would not let her. However, he did not use force to restrain her, and so it was decided that she could have come, and not having done so, she was excluded. A discussion about this followed and:

> After consideration it was concluded and resolved, that unless a person was restrained by force, it was no excuse for absenting themselves from the assemblies of the congregation.[6]

The Broadmead Records make it clear that women were exercising a recognized ministry in the church, that of Deaconess, from 1662.[7] The women who were appointed to this had to be widows of at least sixty, who agreed not to remarry.[8] They were charged to care for the sick, not just women but men - this was why they had be over sixty - and to care for the needy, as well as being required to

> speak a word to their soules as occasion requires, for support and consolation, to build them up in a spirituall lively faith in Jesus Christ.

They were set apart with prayer and fasting, recognized by the congregation as having something more than the normal role of church member - they were ministers.

Women also, in some instances at least, spoke in church. Again in Fenstanton, Sister Anne Harriman threatened to withdraw her membership because:

> Brother Naudin had said he would not walk with such as gave liberty to women to speak in church, whilst she, for her part, would not walk where she had not this right.[9]

These and other women found themselves part of a movement which took their place in giving and receiving ministry seriously, even to the extent of cost to themselves and other members of the congregation. Did they experience it as harsh or liberating? Did they find in these fellowships places where, as women, they had a new dignity and authority, or where they exchanged one sort of domination for another? These may be questions we should like to ask them, but they are not questions they can answer for us, since these are not terms and ideas they would use. What we can see are women who took their own consciences and beliefs seriously and who found fellowships where this was respected. They had their own relationship with God, in some instances in opposition to their husbands and therefore contravening their authority, normally backed up by appeal to the order of God. They were, some of them, in exceptional circumstances, able to preach, and became famous, or notorious for it. They were ministered to with seriousness and expected to respond. Theirs was not a religion of comfort or sentimentality - nor was it one for the women and children, while men got on with real life. Here were women who received and gave ministry within fellowships who knew themselves to be the churches of Christ in a lost world.

In 1685, James the Second of England came to the throne, a Roman Catholic. The Duke of Monmouth led a rebellion, in which many dissenters were involved. It was put down with great ferocity, by Judge Jefferies. Some of those who escaped hid in London and the King was particularly concerned to find those who had harboured the rebels. One was Elizabeth Gaunt. Ivimey quotes Bishop Burnet's version of the story:

There was in London one Gaunt, a woman that was an Anabaptist, who spent a great part of her life in acts of charity, visiting the jails, and looking after the poor of what persuasion soever they were. One of the rebels found her out, and she harboured him in her house, and was looking for the occasion to send him out of the kingdom. He went about in the night and heard what the king had said. So he by an unheard-of baseness went and delivered himself and accused her that had harboured him. She was seized on and tried. There was no witness to prove that she knew the person she harboured was a rebel, except he himself. Her maid witnessed only that he was entertained at her house; but though her crime was that of harbouring a traitor, and was proved only by this infamous witness, yet the judge charged the jury to bring her in guilty, pretending that the maid was a second witness, though she knew nothing of that which was the criminal part. She was condemned and burnt, as the law directs in women convicted of treason. She died with a constancy, even to cheerfulness, that struck all who saw it. She said, charity was a part of her religion as well as faith; this at worst was feeding an enemy. So she hoped that she had reward with him for whose sake she did this service, how unworthy soever the person was who made so ill a return for it. She rejoiced that God had honoured her to be the first that suffered by fire in this reign, and that her suffering was a martyrdom for that religion which was all love. Pen the Quaker told me that he saw her die. She laid the straw about her for burning her speedily and behaved herself in such a manner that all the spectators melted in tears.

Elizabeth Gaunt was executed on October 23 1685.

There is a pattern in religious movements which appears to occur in most and is certainly clear amongst Baptists: as a movement grows in acceptability and respectability, so it becomes a recognizable institution with structures, patterns and expectations. This is necessary for survival. But it has a cost, and much of the cost is paid by women, since the growth of institutionalization in almost every case leads to a more restricted role for women within the organization. This can be seen to be true in the early church, in the reform movements of the fourth century, the twelfth century and the sixteenth century. It certainly appears to be the case as the Baptists move from the heady and dangerous days of the seventeenth century in to the quieter and somewhat more respectable days of the eighteenth century. In the writings and records of the time about church life, it is not clear that women were taking part in the same ways - what seems to be happening is that stricter rules are being applied not only to women speaking in church worship, but also in church meeting. Women seem no longer to have the vote or the possibility of taking part in making decisions. What the women were doing was writing, especially hymns, but also autobiographies and accounts of the action of grace in their lives. In doing this, they were still able to take part in the communal expression of the life of the fellowship - to bear a part in the ministry of and to the church, but in patterns that had become more respectable, and therefore more restrictive.

For Baptists, the eighteenth century, starting with the glorious revolution of 1688 was a time of freedom, of consolidation and - in some parts of the two movements at least - of stagnation. The Particular Baptists became deeply marked by hyper-Calvinism, the Generals by a tendency towards Unitarianism. In the wider Christian world, the middle and end of the century were marked by revival, especially the rise of Methodism. Revival, it was sourly noted, appealed particularly to women:

I have heard Mr Wesley remark that more women are converted than men, and I believe that by far the greatest part of his people are female, and not a few of them sour, disappointed old maids ...[10]

Women were not only converted but they preached, as evangelists and teachers. But, again, this was outside the institution, on the edges, impelled by a particular calling - a form of ministry recognized because it was charismatic, not because it was institutional. Wesley, unhappy about women preaching in his infant movement, rationalized it thus:

> The Lord blesses their preaching and people are converted.
> Who am I to stand against God?

But he remained unhappy about the principle and, following his death, as the movement took a less one-man centred form, the preaching of women was suppressed.

What of the Baptists in this? On the whole, they were not overly enamoured of revival. Until the New Connexion under Dan Taylor became part of the movement - and even after - there was quite a suspicion, especially among the hyper-Calvinists, concerned to do nothing which would undermine the sovereign action of God.

But the women wrote hymns. In their hymns, we can see something of the ministry, in its widest sense, which they offered to their fellow-Baptists, and also something of their experience of being ministered to.

Anne Steele came from a well-established Baptist family in Broughton, a village in Hampshire. Born in 1716, she was to marry, aged twenty-one, when, the day before her wedding, her fiancé was drowned. She had always been frail and sickly, and this was not to improve, but she lived until 1778, although she was bedridden for the last few years. She wrote

hymns and poems on religious subjects, published as Poems on subjects chiefly devotional, *over the name 'Theodosia'.*
  Carey Bonner writes:

> *In an age when Paul's stern saying 'I suffer not a woman to teach ... but to be in silence' was literally and rigidly enforced [a woman] dared to hymn the praises of [her] Redeemer, using a pen-name ... Anne Steele, a great invalid; she learned in suffering what she taught in song.*[11]

Dr Louis Benson wrote of her:

> *Exchanging the common ground for the feminine standpoint, she gave us the Hymn of Introspection and of intense devotion to Christ's person, expressed in terms of heightened emotion. She added to English Hymnody the plaintive sentimental note.*[12]

After her death, her hymns were published in three volumes, with a memoir by Caleb Evans of Bristol, and for several generations remained among the staples of Baptist worship. Writing in 1962, Hugh Martin said: 'She was the first woman to make a real and lasting contribution to hymnody.[13]

Hymns were not the only means of expression open through the pen. There were those who wrote of God's dealing in their lives and of their own understanding of it. Such a one was Ann Dutton, who published, amongst almost fifty other books, three volumes of her autobiography, which in this context are particularly important in giving something of her perception of being ministered to. Ann Dutton records in the story of her life how she moved several times because of the work of her two husbands - when the first died, she married within a few years. Each time, what was important to her was to find a fellowship where she would be properly ministered to - indeed, in at least two cases, it was she who initiated the move for precisely that reason. A Particular Baptist, she records her admiration for Mr Skepp, under whose ministry she sat in London. She wrote praising him for:

> his Quickness of Thought, Aptness of Expression, suitable Affection and a most agreeable Delivery ... his Ministry abounded in Similies ... the Special Blessing I received under it was the more abundant Life and Power of Truths known.

Clearly for Dutton, good ministry was that which taught and encouraged in the understanding of the faith. In this she was at one with many of her Particular Baptist contemporaries, in an era when the minutiae of doctrinal correctness was as important as the fervour of faith.

Dr Whitley commented that 'She aspired to be the Countess of Huntington of the Baptist Denomination';[14] writing of her in 1946, H. Wheeler Robinson said:

> We are conscious of the narrowness and the provincialism of her outlook, her misuse of Scripture as a Delphic oracle to confirm her own desires, the unpleasant sentimentality of her use of Canticles, her conspicuous egoism. On the other hand, we ought to recognise that some at least of these faults belong to her age rather than peculiarly to herself.[15]

While not wanting to disagree with the suggestion that these faults were as much of Dutton's generation as of her personality, I also want to suggest that they were at least in part produced because she was a woman in a situation in which she could not develop, explore and use the gifts which, had she been a man, would have been recognized, and channelled into formal ministry.

Here we begin to touch on some of the pain of the story of women and ministry in Baptist life - those women who, being told and believing that the gifts and willingness that they have can be used only in certain ways and not in others because of their gender, find themselves in the impossible and painful situation of having either to deny the way God has made, shaped and called them, or the fellowship, background and beliefs which give them their context and sense of being. I suggest that Ann Dutton was one of these - one of the lucky ones, since she had the expression of the pen - but that she was far from alone, then or now.

Of course, the high-Calvinism of the Particular Baptists and the drift to unitarianism of the some of the General Baptists were not the only features of eighteenth-century Baptist life. Just as the New Connexion reinvigorated the possibility of General Baptist life, so the moderate Calvinism of the Evans of the Bristol Academy, of Fuller and of Carey brought new life to the Particular Baptists, and, in the case of Fuller and Carey, brought the founding of the Baptist Missionary Society - another form of ministry within the Baptist movement, that of overseas service, preaching, teaching, church planting, and eventually medical and agricultural work. This was to prove a very important area for women in terms of ministry, both overseas and at home, in support and organization.

The name most associated with the early work of women in the BMS is Hannah Marshman, who went with her husband as one of the first to work in Serampore. Involved from the beginning in educational work, she was recognized as 'the first woman missionary in India'.   Stanley, however, points out that:

> The active role of Hannah Marshman in the Serampore Mission may have been unique in its day, but it is possible that later missionary wives did as much, but without the public recognition that she received.[16]

Indeed, Brian Stanley has in his library a book called *The Life and Labours of a Congo Pioneer*, by W. Holman Bentley, which has as its frontispiece a photograph with the title 'The First Four Missionaries to the Congo; Holman Bentley; HE Crudgington; JS Hartland; TJ and Mrs Comber' - four missionaries, five people. Again and again, the women who take part in offering ministry in its various forms are silenced and painted out - even when they are there!

In 1781, William Carey married his master's sister-in-law, Dorothy, an illiterate woman. When he started to speak of the possibility of service overseas, Dorothy was not enamoured of the prospect, and refused to go. William decided to go anyway, taking his eldest son, Felix, with him, and leaving the rest. The first attempt ended prematurely when they could get no further than Portsmouth. At the next attempt, having given birth to another child just three weeks previously, Dorothy agreed to go, with all the children. The first settlement was in malarial swamps, where Dorothy and the two oldest boys were constantly ill. Following some time in Calcutta, they moved to Malda where William was foreman in an indigo factory - and where Dorothy was becoming more and more physically and mentally ill. In 1794, their five-year-old son died, and she lost her grip on sanity. Co-workers described her as 'wholly deranged'. William continued to work in the factory, to spend hours translating, to preach and to set up schools. In 1800, the family moved to Serampore, where the missionaries lived in community. William continued to preach, to translate, to set up a college and to work with the other missionaries. John Marshman wrote of how he worked on his translations, 'while an insane wife frequently wrought up to a state of most distressing excitement was in the next room ...' She died in 1807, aged fifty-one. A writer in this century has written:

> *It was no doubt a relief to Carey. She had long since ceased to be a useful member of the mission family. In fact, she was a hindrance to the work.*

The area where women's ministry offered through the missionary movement really came into its own was in the Zenana Missions - work amongst the women who were kept in seclusion. Obviously such work could only be done by women, and it became the women's work at home to organize this as well. This movement, which at first went under the wonderful title of 'The Ladies Association for the Support of Zenana Work and Bible Women in Connection with the Baptist Missionary Society', later shortened to the Baptist Zenana Mission, began through the work of the wives of missionaries in India, and then moved into sending its own missionaries - the first a Miss Fryer of Bristol, and employing Indian women, and also extended its work to China. This became both a blessing and a difficulty for women who wanted to offer ministry in this way - there was a place here to work - but it became the only place. Stanley says:

> Throughout the period [the nineteenth century] the BMS remained a predominantly male society, staffed and controlled almost entirely by men.[17]

The BZM on the other hand was an almost entirely female operation - an area of independence and ministry. In 1910, at an international missionary conference in Edinburgh, it came to be felt that the rationale for separate women's movements was no longer strong, and so BZM was incorporated into BMS - and into the male structure. Thus, at the beginning of the twentieth century, one of the avenues of recognized women's service in the Baptist movement was closed down.

But other things were changing too in the twentieth century, and other forms of ministry were appearing, including admission to the ordained ministry, the recognized pastorate within the denomination, as well as, for part of this time, a specific female form of ministry in the form of the Deaconess movement.

The Deaconess Order was set up in 1890, as a Baptist response to the same impulse which had started the Anglican Deaconess order in 1862. Doris Rose in her history of the movement, written in 1954, speaks of a need to train women to respond to moral and social decline, people who could go into homes:

> To brighten the lives of men, women and children and most of all to win them to Jesus Christ.[18]

The first pattern was that the sisters lived together under a Lady Superintendent. From this centre, they ran a Medical Mission, a Mothers' Meeting and a Christmas club. The sisters got involved in day-to-day social care of families in the slum.

In 1919, the Union took over the running of the Order and set up the first College, which gave training in a range of theological and practical work, from New Testament

Greek to first aid. The deaconess also undertook placements, including Sunday School work, speaking to women's meetings, welfare and medical mission work.

In the 'twenties, the pattern changed again. Now sisters found themselves called on to help build up causes which were suffering from lack of leadership. In 1928, The Lancashire and Cheshire Association appointed an Itinerant Sister to work with the weaker churches - a appointment which continued until 1954.

Although the College moved and greatly changed its shape in 1929, it was providing more than was being looked for. In the 'thirties, deaconesses began to be appointed to pastor mission churches and start new work, and in 1938 the movement became part of the Women's Department of the Union.

By now something rather strange was going on. A report in 1941 said:

> We do not aim at training women ministers, but some deaconesses have been virtually put in the position of ministers and have been given the responsibility of organising and maintaining churches ... Their work is of a real missionary character, but the denomination appears slow to appreciate the vital need and importance of this work that is being done in the field at their very gates.

By the late 'forties, an increasing number of the deaconesses were being called to accept the full charge of small churches or to establish and build up new ones. They were acting as pastors, often in very difficult circumstances, and were not given the recognition - or pay - that the 'ministers' were given.

The Baptist Home Mission for Scotland was struggling in the 1930s to find suitable ministry for the highland and island, Gaelic-speaking churches. Mary Flora MacArthur, whose father was a minister, was called as pastor to the church in Tobermory from 1938-1941, having served as an evangelist among the fisher-girls in Lerwick in the earlier 'thirties. She then became the missionary at Eday and Sanday in Orkney from 1943-1945, and was pastor on Colonsay from 1945-47.

Nor was she inventing the wheel for the first time. In 1913, Jane Henderson, a deaconess from Stirling, led missions to Shetland and the north-east, again amongst fisher-people. In 1918, she was called to the pastorate in Lossiemouth, where she served until 1921, and from where she continued to travel to lead missions.

By the mid-60s, there were forty active deaconesses, of whom thirty-eight were functioning as pastors. This had developed partly because of men being away in the forces: it was one of those things which grew up rather than had a decision made about it. Various changes in organization had taken place, which placed Deaconesses on more of a par with ministers in terms of recognition - but they were still paid less, and still required, until 1967, to resign on marrying.

In 1975, the Council decided that, in the light of falling numbers and in view of the anomalies which had arisen, recruitment to the Order would be suspended, and all active deaconesses would be transferred to the ministerial list: one colleague speaks of the direction which came to 'get revved up'. This was possible because, by 1975, women were listed along with men on the list of accredited ministers.

Because of our ecclesiology and lack of a central body making binding decisions, Baptists tend to work with a pattern that things are first done pragmatically and then reasoned out theologically - like the dramatic increase of deaconesses in pastoral charge. The same thing happened over women being accepted as ministers of local churches.

In 1918, Edith Gates was called as the pastor of Little Tew and Cleverly in Oxfordshire. Once there, after passing the Baptist Union examinations, for those entering ministry without a time of training in one of the colleges, she was put on the list as a probationer minister in 1922. Maria Living-Taylor was also accepted as a probationer in 1922, and served in a joint pastorate with her husband. Three years later, both were transferred to the main list - or at least to the equivalent of the main list. There was actually a separate list for women ministers and probationers in the handbook until 1966. From 1927 until 1956 they were listed as 'Women Pastors', and then until 1966 as 'Women Ministers'.

In 1925, faced with the reality of women serving in the recognized ministry, the Baptist Union Council set up a committee which produced a report stating that 'Baptists see no objection to women ministers' - which was just as well, as Baptists by now had women ministers!

In 1922 the first woman was accepted for training in a Baptist College. Bristol had agreed to allow it in 1919, but no women had applied. In 1922, Violet Hedger, who felt a call to missionary service, applied to Spurgeon's but was turned down since the College did not accept women. Instead she was accepted at Regent's Park College, by the then Principal, Dr Gould. Unfortunately, by the time she arrived, there was a new principal, Wheeler Robinson, who did not approve of her presence and did his best to ignore it. The custom at this time was that the principal paid the examination fees for the students - but not for Violet

Hedger who, having paid her own fees, graduated and served local churches until her retirement.

In 1925 there were two accredited women ministers in England. In 1965 there were five: two in pastoral charge, one of whom, in 1967, became the first woman to stay in ministry after her marriage - to another minister[19].

In 1965, there were sixty-one accredited and active deaconesses, most of whom were in pastoral charge.

In the *Fraternal* magazine in 1961 Gwenyth Hubble, who was in charge of deaconess training, wrote:

> I am driven therefore, to conclude that the existence of an order of deaconesses has been, for us as a denomination, an escape route by which we have avoided facing the real issue of women in the pastoral ministry, and we have been content, because of the shortage of male ministers, to let women do the work of the pastoral ministry and call them by another name.[20]

The numbers of women in pastoral ministry as recognized ministers began to rise sharply in the 'seventies: in 1970 there were 23, and in 1992, the latest year for which I have figures, there were 102 women out of a total of 2187 ministers. Of these 102 women, 58 were in pastorate, 32 working alone and 26 in teams. Seven were doing other denominational jobs: one an association secretary, two college tutors, one with the BMS, one warden and two on the Baptist Union staff. Eight were working for other Christian organizations, twenty-two were retired and seven out of pastorate.

In 1967 the Baptist Union Council received a report, *Women in the Service of the Denomination* (have we ever had a report on men in the service of the denomination?), which affirmed:

All the privileges and responsibilities of Christian discipleship are open to men and women alike. Moreover, the presence and guidance of the Lord, the Spirit, is promised to the Church for the ordering of its life and the fulfilment of its mission.[21]

and

The Committee believes that witness-bearing and ministry are the continuing responsibility of the whole Church; that within this general responsibility, particular individuals should be set aside for special tasks; and that there are no grounds of principle or doctrine for debarring women duly qualified from any of the special forms of ministry.[22]

We have had no women Superintendents, no woman has been head of a department of the Union and only two women have served as President of the Union. In 1995-96, out of 225 members of Council, there are forty-two women.

Neil Hall in his research, *Waiting in the Wings*, has shown how, although there are no rules or regulations to prevent women from taking posts in association life, it just does not seem to happen somehow. There are all sorts of ways in which women are made unable to take responsibility or leadership.

Keith Jones has written about it like this:

I regret that we have not had the deep debate some other traditions have had about the place of leadership of women. Baptists in England 'slid' into ordaining women in ministry early this century, but if we are honest there are still far too many no-go areas for women, and we are impoverished, I believe, by not having the insights of some of our very gifted women ministers on the Board of the General Superintendents, more frequent women presidents and more women in senior staff positions with our associations and Union.[23]

In 1910, a Miss Clark of Glasgow, who was in the first year of her Arts degree, wrote to J.H. Shakespeare. She explained that in the following year she would also be reading Divinity, and within three years would have both her MA and her BD. She was asking whether, having done that, she could be recognized as a Baptist student. The committee replied that they could not consider the case of anybody 'not actually engaged in pastoral work', and the matter was closed.[24]

On the structural side in England, there has been a long history of women's work, enabling women, and run by women. The Baptist Women's Home Work Auxiliary became the Baptist Women's League in 1910, and was very active. It was backed up, in 1938, by the opening of the Women's Department of the Union, which survived until the 'eighties. BWL itself came to an end in the early 1980s, and was replaced by the Women's Mission Network. Again, we have to ask, is this not another example of a structural marginalization? That is not to question the importance and impact of the work of such organizations, but to ask important questions about structures which necessitate them.

As this survey has shown, both women and ministry have been fluctuating categories through our story, but they have both been present, at times and in different shapes, together. The very telling of the story raises questions, some of which I have indicated as I have gone along. Some of the questions are to do with structures. If women are finding it so difficult to take part in the structures, can and should this be changed, and if so how? Some are to do with our understanding of ministry. What language can we find to describe and affirm the ministry that women have always offered in care, support, encouragement and being there?

I want, however, in this part of my discussion, to ask some different questions.

Violet Hedger reported being told by a friend that she

> had come to a service out of curiosity and said it was alright once you got used to the difference.[25]

- in this context largely a difference of sight - seeing a woman in the pulpit - and of sound - hearing a female rather than a male voice. This was chiefly in the context of a service, but not only there; in the wider context differences were deeper and more subtle.

Here we strike one of the big questions in discussing women and ministry: is there a difference between the ministry of women and the ministry of men? At this point, I must confess to profound feelings of ambiguity. Having had the experience of being assured that my ministry, though no less valuable than a man's, is of a different order - which is to say, that it is not appropriate for me to preach - I am rather suspicious of the 'different but equal' description. It seems to me that it has been used to define, or rather to limit, what is appropriate or possible for women - that is, for all women as a class, not individual women - while not creating a corresponding definition for men. I have been arguing through this lecture that this type of limitation has not worked fully, but, when it has been at its most effective, then there has been suffering for women and for the church. 'Equal but different' has been used to mean different and so (for women) inferior. I have argued and continue to argue very strongly that the use of such a phrase in itself helps to perpetuate inequality.

The most commonly cited difference between women and men is the affective one: women, whether by nature or socialization, are directed towards feeling, relationship and collaborative working, while men's focus is more on action, thinking and competition. These, of course, are generalizations, even caricatures, but they are often the characteristics cited in discussion about ministry. It may well be that this is one of the more obvious differences that women's ministry will point out. But since it is quite obvious that many men also express their ministry through feeling, relationship and collaboration, while there are women who show the features of action, thinking and competition, it is my contention that these are surface issues and there are much more profound issues in question here.

This is not say that the category of difference is unimportant, but I want to locate that category in another place. The difference that matters in this discussion is not between men and women ontologically - in their being - but contextually - the way in which we experience the world, and the patterns that world sets up for us.

Firstly there is the question of ontological identity. This is the apparently obvious assertion that men and women exist in the same way, that they are the same species: indeed, that women as well as men are made in the image of God. This is an apparently obvious assertion, but one which has not always been accepted as such. We live in the Christian church as a community which has at times denied this assertion, sometimes in words, and more often in action. While our theology now, normally, does not allow us to suggest that women are not made in the image of God, are not human in the way that men are human, we still live with the reality that it can be asserted, in a discussion about women in ministry, that men represent the divine and women the human.[26] This implies that therefore men are somehow more perfect, more in the image of God than women. There are a whole series of consequences which flow from such an understanding, not only to do with the ministry of women, though there are profound consequences for any discussion of that, but also to do with our perception of the nature of God. Mary Daly phrased it thus: 'If God is male, then male is God.' There are consequences too for our perception of the world. If men and women are so different symbolically, in 'meaning', then a world shaped by, for and through men, with women on the margins as a subset who do not quite fit, is a perfectly appropriate form of structure.

My contention, however, is that we need to take seriously the Creation reality that: 'in the image of God God created them, male and female God created them', and also the baptismal reality that 'as many of you as are baptized into Christ have put on Christ. There is no longer Jew or Greek, slave or free, male or female, but you are all one in Christ Jesus.' This baptismal formula does not mean, as has been argued, that as far as God is concerned we are all free Jewish men[27], but that the distinctions which have been used by the world to discriminate in terms of status and worth have no place in the life of the Christian church. Men and women exist before God in the same way - created, redeemed and baptized.

This assertion was fundamental to the early Baptists: that in the light of baptism, all believers were in an equal position before God, and so there was no priestly caste, no hierarchical authority, but a priesthood of all believers who together sought the will of God for the people of God, who worshipped together as a body, and who covenanted to walk together in mutual care and support.

For those early Baptists, this insistence on the equality of baptismal position was at the root of their insistence that women were members of the church, that women could vote, that women had a part in the ministry. I want to argue that we must keep on developing an understanding of ministry which grows out of our convictions about baptism. The fundamental position which we hold is that of a baptized believer, a member of God's church. Everything else is a consequence of that. If baptism is such a radically equalizing gift, then we have questions to ask about anything within our communal life which denies that equalizing experience.

I have asserted, however, that difference is present, and I want to maintain that this difference is one of context. I do not mean this in a simplistic way which would suggest that, if only men and women were educated the same and had equal opportunities in the workplace, then we would reach perfection. The context to which I am referring is much broader than simply our day-to-day living. It is the context of a history which has said continually and sometimes violently that men are of intrinsic worth and women's worth is at best derived from theirs, and at worst is non-existent. It is a context which has functioned with the symbolism of a link between male and rational, female and irrational, male and spiritual, female and physical. It is a context which, even now, will look to women to carry the affective role in a community, while men are expected to be logical and unaffected by feelings - an expectation which is often reflected in our understanding of women in ministry: that a woman will be particularly good at pastoral work, for example, while a man's gifts will normally lie in teaching and leading. Such a context is not simply one of expectation, but carries with it a force of creation - women are trained, expected, guided into and moulded as the bearers of a community's feelings, while men are fitted for leadership and so on.

We inevitably experience the world in a context: we do not deal in unmediated experiences. The whole of our faith is an assertion of this. God does not come to us out of nowhere, but in the being of a particular man at a particular time, doing and saying particular things. This context is so much part of us, that it takes a bit of work to question it. However, I believe that it is important that we do. We are charged not to be conformed to the world, but to be transformed in the renewing of our minds - which involves, among other things, asking questions about assumptions.

One of the questions we need to ask is not 'can women "do" this?' in terms of ministry, but 'what is ministry?' in the light of our assertions about baptism and the nature of the Christian community.

If we are going to take seriously our theology of the baptized status as the primary status of every believer, then this must have its consequences for our understanding of ministry - and indeed, it has had. Refusing to adopt a model which we pejoratively refer to as 'the priestly caste', we have worked throughout our history, not always successfully, at trying to find another understanding of ministry. Committed to the theology that ministry is a gift of God which at its root is exercised by the whole church, and within which particular functions are carried out by those called by God through God's free choice, we have refused to limit ministry to those hierarchically ordained. For most of our story, however, we have acknowledged the importance of recognizing the call of God through some form of ordination or commissioning, even if we have not all always been sure exactly what we mean by ordination. Looking to God to give the gifts of ministry, we have insisted that the call and gifting of God is primary and without that there can be no ministry. At times we have been so suspicious of interfering with these gifts, or of attempting to create them where God has not given them that we have doubted the worth of intellectual training (while having the oldest continuing Dissenting College in the world!). We have insisted theologically that the minister's role is contained within that of Church Meeting, that it is together that we seek the will of God, while acknowledging that within that setting, the minister plays a particular role of leadership, teaching, vision and encouragement. Our ministry has its grounding in our sense of the Church as a local gathered community to such an extent that we will not ordain anybody who has not been commended by a local church, and moreover we insist that the calling is confirmed by an invitation to a local pastorate. Together with that, we recognize and work for the interdependence of our fellowships, acknowledged in England by a nationally recognized list of ministers - so ministry is not entirely local, but is also more widely shared. We stand very firmly on the responsibility of the local church to call its own minister without let or hindrance from elsewhere, though we may have lost something of the richness of our past, when an Association of churches was involved in helping an individual fellowship and an individual minister discern God's will.

So, in all this, our understanding of ministry is based on the primary calling signified and actualized in baptism, and is worked out in service through the gathered community of believers.

However, in the practice of this theology, we live in a context, and it is appropriate that we should reflect on that context, and the part it plays in the pattern that ministry assumes among us. This means we must question the fundamental social functioning of our world, and come to terms with the fact that it is deeply patriarchal.

The power of patriarchy is not simply to do with who gets what job, or the injustice of female poverty. It is a way of defining the world which claims that the male is norm and all else is deviance. In 1985, Schussler Fiorenza wrote:

> ... androcentric scholarship defines women as the 'other' of man or of a male God and reduces us to 'objects' of male scholarship ... Far from being objective or descriptive, androcentric texts and knowledge maintain the silence and invisibility engendered by a patriarchal society and Church.[28]

This explains more clearly than I can the problem I have with this topic: to talk about women and ministry is immediately to define women as other. It is also impossible. We can only talk about women and men and ministry, because it is together that we give and receive ministry, just as together we are created in the image of God.

In a book discussing the image of God, Joan Aldredge Clanton writes:

> ... the woman question is also a man question, and ultimately a God question.[29]

To say that we function in a patriarchal context is not only to make a judgement, but also to put content into my assertion earlier that the difference between men and women, and so between the ministry of men and women, lies in context. Men function and experience differently in a patriarchal context which affirms male as normal and ascribes intrinsic worth to masculinity - this is different from women in such a context, categorized as abnormal and with their worth linked to other issues. For both men and women the experience may be comfortable or uncomfortable, but whichever it is, it will not be the same. That patriarchy is now named and recognized as not being inherent in the way the world is at least raises the possibility of asking questions, but has not yet significantly changed the reality. This is obviously a very wide - indeed, all-encompassing - issue which I cannot consider fully here. But I want to raise it as a context in which we consider, practice and experience ministry. While we still talk of women and ministry as a separate issue - indeed, while we still have women's work as separate from the 'assumed' work of the organization, we are working in a patriarchal pattern, which will deny women the right to be recognized as normal, as real and as the image of God. Simply to ordain women into ministry on the same basis as men, in the same mould as men, will not change this. To do that is to ask women to be men, irrespective of the difference in context within which they function and are perceived by others - a rather pointless exercise.

I want to draw extensively on Sara Maitland's book, *Map of a New Country*, for the next part of my argument, because she argues the case particularly clearly and coherently. She points out early in her argument that:

What Protestant women have conclusively proved ... is that they can work and are determined to work, within a range of Christian ministries ... but that this in itself has not solved the problem of sexism within Christianity[30]

She then goes on to point out that:

> The recent history of women in institutional Christianity proves only that ordination itself does not solve any problems ... It may in a subtle way make it *harder* for other women to lay claim to their own vocation, because the most obvious charge of discrimination is eliminated. All institutions with histories as long as Christianity's are accomplished in the art of co-opting dissident factions ... The clerical model is a very old and very powerful one. By inviting some of the most able and enthusiastic women into its power structures, institutional Christianity may be able to evade the more profound issues of in-built sexism and dualism.[31]

Pointing out that women in ministry often take their definition of 'proper ministry' from the male role model which has contributed to their oppression, she goes on to make a profoundly important point about the difference women in ministry can make:

> Christian women can, if we make institutional Christianity listen to us, make a special contribution to the evolution of Christian structures precisely because of our experience of being outside ...[32]

She finishes with the reminder that 'Moses did not organize a campaign to be next Pharaoh'.[33]

If Maitland is right, if women do have something important and distinctive to bring to ministry, surely this is where it must lie. It is not that women do certain things better than men, not that women are more caring, or nicer, or even represent other areas of the being of God. What women bring is a different context in which ministry is experienced and expressed - which may therefore mean that certain women do some things better than certain men, or that other understandings of God become important. But this emerges not out of their being women, but out of the context in which we learn to function socially and emotionally, a context shaped fundamentally by patriarchy, and therefore the experience of oddity, alienation and marginalization which results from that.

Women may do the same things as men, but because of the context out of which they act, and from which they are perceived, it will be a different experience for both the woman and for those receiving her ministry. An example of the way in which this is true in preaching is discussed in *Silence in Heaven*, an anthology of women's preaching. In the introduction, the editors write:

> The woman who preaches can assume much less about her own position and tradition in which she stands than her male colleagues. As many of us have been made acutely aware, merely to speak from the body of a woman is to present a challenge to some congregations. An entirely conventional sermon may take on new resonances as it is delivered by a person whose body presents an unconventional icon of authority.[34]

Maitland comments that Moses did not organize a campaign to be the next Pharaoh. Instead, to take her notion further, he turned his back on the stultifying structures of Egypt, which kept his people in slavery, and set out with as many of them as would come across a harsh, demanding and unsafe desert to reach the Land of Milk and Honey. There are those who argue that this is the

only way forward for women. Some, like Mary Daly and
Daphne Hampson, who understand the whole faith to be so
deeply patriarchal that women can have no place in it, have
moved outside the Christian community altogether. Others
have set up or become involved in women-only
congregations, arguing that reformation from within is not
possible. This has even been suggested from within our
own community as the only way forward for women's
ministry. Anthony Barker, in his MTh Thesis 'Women's
Roles in Baptist Churches', presents this as a way forward.
He describes his vision thus:

> Such churches [Womanist Baptist Churches] would include
> men, but would ensure that women were dominant,
> especially lay-women who would hold all the key
> responsibilities ... Only women would teach and preach,
> so that female images, illustration and language would
> become normal in congregational life.[35]

Still others, and this is the category into which I come,
have suggested by action if not word that Moses in fact got
it wrong, and becoming the next Pharaoh was exactly what
he should have done. We have become part of the
structures. We are aware that the fit is not always good, but
we work, on the good days, to change the structures and,
on the bad days, to change ourselves, so that the rubbing
will not leave us too raw. And there have been times when
our arguments for change have made a difference - the
acceptance of guidelines for maternity leave, for example
(though be it noted, we argued for paternity leave too, but
this was unacceptable). The fact remains that, for the most
part, we have been co-opted into the structures. Whether
this is good or bad, I make no judgement, being part of the
category I describe. But if we take seriously, as

we should, Maitland's comment that the important and distinctive thing which women bring to ministry as women, quite apart from the particular gifts which each woman brings, is outsideness, then if we slot ourselves into the structures we are in danger of denying that. Our movement is in danger of ignoring this gift, if the structures, as opposed to the ministry, become the place we look for the gift of God to the Church.

One of the things which being on the outside can mean is that the constraints that are placed on insiders do not - or at least need not - apply. To go back to preaching as an example, Goldingay has pointed out that preaching and person have always interacted:

> As Brooks ... famously put it more than a century ago, preaching is proclamation through personality. A disembodied preacher cannot credibly proclaim the incarnate Christ ... No preacher can grab us by the entrails who is not in touch with his or her own humanity.[36]

He then goes on:

> Troeger [in *Effective Preaching*] suggests that in North America a 'homiletic of personal authenticity for the pulpit' is emerging through the impact of women clergy. In Britain, my limited experience suggests that women are as inhibited as are men in being themselves in preaching, as in other contexts they seem as reserved as men in owning their feelings, perhaps because we have required them to behave like honorary men. But perhaps the ordination of women to the priesthood might give new impetus both to women and men towards such authenticity in life, ministry and preaching.

Well, perhaps. Or perhaps that will only come when the outsider's voice is heard as that of an outsider, and valued for that, rather than being translated and rewritten to fit accepted patterns. If the ministry of women is to be taken seriously, then it is not simply a question of accepting women into the existing structures - though all honour must be paid to those who have stuck it out within them - but also a radical questioning of the way we structure ministry, train for it and the expectations we put onto it.

In this discussion I have attempted to tell the stories of some of the women who have offered, thought about and received ministry in a small area of Baptist history. I believe it is important that these stories are heard for their own sake, for two reasons. Firstly, they give us a place to stand, those of us who are women doing the same things today - we do not have to reinvent the wheel, it is already in existence. If we are going to ask the questions I am asking for, then we need this safe place.

Secondly, one of the experiences that is common to many women is of being used for someone else's benefit, be it physically, emotionally or symbolically. I am trying not to use these women, but simply to tell their stories.

Inevitably we draw conclusions and make patterns from the stories and from what is not said. That women have made judgements about ministry has been a regular feature of our common story. That women have offered ministry in various forms, usually around the edges, has also become clear. For the past perhaps three generations, ministry of women has, in some measure at least, been present among us in a formal recognized sense. We have done what Maitland has outlined and invited women into the structures - without notable changes to the deep structures. Some of us have adapted to the patriarchal hegemony better than others, but for almost all of us there has been some degree of pain. Perhaps the very ease with which some of us have adapted has, as Maitland warns, made it harder for others to claim their vocation (while those of us who are absorbed may be denying the pain of our own) - to be the voice from the margins, the unconventional pattern, the questioning of the way things are.

To be on the outside or the edge is an uncomfortable position: it causes discomfort for the one who is there, because of the sense of exclusion, powerlessness and strangeness, and it also causes discomfort for those on the inside, if they are willing to be aware of it, because it is the reminder that theirs is not the only way of looking at the universe, of understanding truth, of living. Because of the discomfort it is often something which we try to avoid - those on the outside try to get in, to feel normal; those on the inside, if they cannot drive the outsider out of existence, try to welcome them in to consolidate their hegemony. This is exactly what has happened with the ministry of women. We exist in a patriarchal context, and there is little indication that this is about to change fundamentally. So, women's experience, from which they take definition and out of which they minister, will continue to be that of outsider, of 'other'. Moses did not organize a campaign to be the next Pharaoh, but went into the desert and existed on the margins. I do not believe and I hope I need never come to believe that we need to exist as a separate 'women's church'. That would be a failure and a denial of the wholeness of the body of Christ.

But if we are going to live with, in and through the ministry of women - not as a problem, not as a concession and not expecting women to deny their context and pretend to be men - then we need to listen to the voices from the margins, accept the ministry offered from the outside, and discover God on the outside, the God who was crucified outside the city wall.

NOTES

1. Adrienne Rich, *On Lies, Secrets and Silence*, London 1980, p.11.
2. K. Thomas, 'Women and the Civil War Sects', *Past and Present*, 13 (1958), p.46.
3. R. Ashton, ed., *John Robinson Works*, London 1851, Vol.II, p.158.
4. R. Hayden, ed., *The records of A Church of Christ in Bristol 1640-1687*, Bristol 1974, pp.87-90.
5. E.B. Underhill, ed., *Records of Churches of Christ gathered at Fenstanton, Warboys and Hexham*, London 1854, p.85.
6. *ibid.*, p.242.
7. Hayden, *op. cit.*, p.117.
8. *ibid.*, p.208.
9. 'She-preachers, Widows and Other Women: The Feminine Dimension in Baptist Life since 1600', John Briggs, *Baptist Quarterly*, vol.31, 1984-85, p.341.
10. J. Lackington, *Memoires of the Forty-Five First Years of the Life of James Lackington*, London 1795, p.72, cited by David Bebbington in *Evangelicalism in Modern Britain: A History from the 1730s to the 1980s*, London 1995, Chap.2 n.51.
11. Carey Bonner, *Some Baptist Hymnists from the Seventeenth Century to Modern Times*, London 1937, p.29.
12. Louis F. Benson, *The English Hymn*, p.214, cited in Bonner.
13. Hugh Martin, 'The Baptist Contribution to Early English Hymnody', *Baptist Quarterly*, vol.19, 1961-62, no.5.
14. Martin, *Baptist Quarterly*, vol.19, no.5.
15. H. Wheeler Robinson, *Life and Faith of the Baptists*, London 1946, p.60.
16. B. Stanley, *The History of the Baptist Missionary Society 1792-1992*, Edinburgh 1992, p.228.
17. *ibid.*, p.232.
18. Doris Rose, *Baptist Deaconesses*, Baptist Union 1954, p.6.

19. Ruth Vinson, who married John Matthews.

20. *Fraternal* 1961, p.14.

21. *Women in the Service of the Denomination*, BUGB 1967, p.3.

22. *ibid.*, p.4.

23. Keith Jones, *Baptist Times*, 4 July 1996, 'What shape the Union?'.

24. Douglas Sparkes, *An Accredited Ministry*, Baptist Historical Society 1996, p.27.

25. *Baptist Quarterly*, vol.10 no.15, 1943, p.246.

26. In an address given at the Glenrothes Assembly in 1997, the Revd J. Graham spoke about issues of women in ministry. In the transcript he supplied of his notes he says:

- the MALE/FEMALE relationship mirrors the DIVINE/HUMAN relationship
- the MALE represents the DIVINE side of the relationship
- the FEMALE represents the HUMAN side of the relationship

NB That is why GOD reveals himself in MALE terms

- He is Father not Mother
  King not Queen
  Husband not Wife

That is why God INCARNATE is Man not Woman.

27. In the same address, Graham examined the text Galatians 3.28 and his notes say:

I   Always the Letter is dealing with VERTICAL relationships not HORIZONTAL relationships

II The CONTEXT has no reference to the ROLES of men and women ...

III This section of the Letter has to do with our INHERITANCE of the blessing promised to Abraham
   - that inheritance can only come through one, Jewish, male descendant of Abraham ...

CONCLUSION So 'in Christ'

there is neither Jew nor Greek	- only JEW
there is neither slave nor free	- only FREE
there cannot be male AND female	- only MALE

and Mr Graham's final statement in his notes is:

Let us together do something magnificent for Jesus by believing that apostolic ends can only be achieved by using apostolic means.

28. 'Breaking the Silence' in *Concilium* 182, 1985, Elizabeth Schussler Fiorenza.

29. Joan Aldredge Clanton, *In Whose Image*, London 1990, p.1.

30. Sara Maitland, *A Map of The New Country; Women and Christianity*, London 1983, p.94.

31. *ibid.*, pp.103-4.

32. *ibid.*, p.128.

33. *ibid.*, p.194.

34. Heather Walton and Susan Durber, eds., *Silence in Heaven*, SCM 1994, pp.xi-xii.

35. Anthony Richard Barker, 'Women's Roles in the Baptist Churches; An Historical and Contemporary Reflection on Baptist Female Leadership in Britain', Thesis for MTh in Applied Theology, University of Oxford. I am very grateful to Mr Barker for allowing me a copy of his thesis.

36. John Goldingay, 'In Preaching Be Scriptural', *Anvil* Vol.14, no. 2, 1997, p.89.